# Rosalynn Carter

## STEEL MAGNOLIA

# Rosalynn Carter

## STEEL MAGNOLIA

### RUTH TURK

## A First Book

FRANKLIN WATTS
*A Division of Grolier Publishing*
New York • London • Hong Kong • Sydney
Danbury, Connecticut

Frontispiece: Rosalynn Carter poses in the White House.
Photographs ©: AP/Wide World Photos: 34, 40, 42, 45, 46;
Jimmy Carter Library: 6, 11, 12, 14, 19, 20, 23;
Reuters/Corbis-Bettmann: 54; Courtesy of Ronald Reagan
Library: 48; UPI/Corbis-Bettmann:
2, 26, 27, 28, 33, 36, 39, 53.

Cover art by Michelle Regan

Library of Congress Cataloging-in-Publication Data

Turk, Ruth, 1917—
Rosalynn Carter: steel magnolia / Ruth Turk
    p.   cm. —(A first book)
Includes bibliographical references and index.
Summary: Presents the life of the former First Lady from
the time of her childhood inPlains, Georgia, through her
years in the White House, and to the present.
ISBN 0—531—20312—3
1. Carter, Rosalynn—Juvenile literature.
2. Presidents' spouses—1924— —Juvenile literature.
[1. Carter, Rosalynn. 2. First ladies. 3. Carter, Jimmy,
1924—.] I. Title. II. Series.
E874.T87  1997
973.926′092—dc21                              96—50025
                                                   CIP
                                                    AC

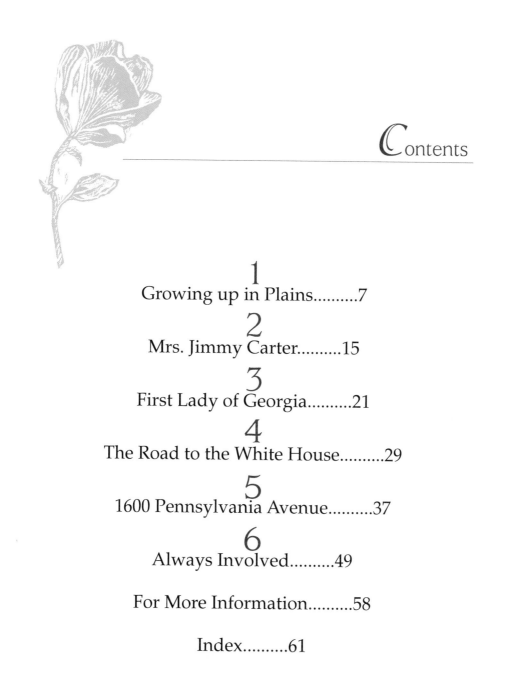

# Contents

*This photograph of Main Street in Plains,
Georgia, shows J. E. Carter's store on the left.
Like Jimmy Carter, Rosalynn grew up in Plains.*

# 1

## $G$rowing up in Plains

Born on August 18, 1927, in the small farming community of Plains, Georgia, Eleanor Rosalynn Smith was the oldest child of Allie Murray and Wilburn Edgar Smith. As the oldest child she soon learned to help her mother with the cooking, cleaning, and other household chores. Rosalynn's brothers, Murray and Jerry, had to milk the cows, feed the pigs, and carry wood for the stove. Later on there would be another daughter in the family, but for now the three children helped their parents as much as possible.

The Smith family was no different from most of the hardworking farm people who lived in Plains. In the 1930s, the population of 683 residents lived within an area of one square mile. The main street had a few stores and a garage, but there was no library, movie theater, or recreation center. Young people met mostly in church or school.

Rosalynn enjoyed going to church. She went to all three churches to which her family belonged: her grandmother's Lutheran church, her grandfather's Baptist church, and her parent's Methodist church. She also went to Sunday school and on weekdays attended prayer meetings and Bible school. In elementary school, Rosalynn studied hard. When she received her first report card with all As, she raced home to show it to her parents. The young student was delighted when her father gave her a whole dollar because that was a generous reward for someone in the first grade in the year 1933.

Rosalynn loved her father very much because he took good care of his family and was fun to be with. He drove a school bus and owned a car repair service.

He was a loving parent who was also strict with his children. Rosalynn was forbidden to cross the street alone because it was dangerous for such a small child. One day, wanting to play with a friend, she crossed the street. Mr. Smith gave her a spanking, then told her not to cry. The little girl minded not being allowed to cry more than being spanked.

After finishing her daily chores, Rosalynn enjoyed reading or cutting out paper dolls. When Mrs. Smith taught her daughter to use a sewing machine, Rosalynn started to make her own clothes. Big city children might have found Rosalynn's life dull, but for the Plains youngster, the mix of school, home, and church activities was never boring.

When Rosalynn was twelve years old, she went to a summer camp for the first time. When she came home, she learned her father had leukemia, a form of cancer. She willingly helped her mother care for her father.

Rosalynn's best friend, Ruth Carter, had a mother who was a registered nurse. Mrs. Carter—everyone called her Miss Lillian—came every day to give the sick man pain injections, but Mr. Smith's condition grew steadily worse. When her father died, Rosalynn was devastated. She realized that her mother needed her help more than ever. While Mrs. Smith sewed clothing for wealthy people, Rosalynn worked at a local beauty shop. In this way she was able to earn some expense money for college.

Graduating from high school as class valedictorian, Rosalynn enrolled at Georgia Southwestern Junior College. Because the school was in the next town of Americus, Rosalynn commuted daily by bus. Her fares and lunches cost $4.50 a week. When she skipped lunch, she was able to save money to see a movie with her friends.

In 1945, while visiting her best friend, Rosalynn fell in love with a picture of Ruth Carter's brother, Jimmy. She had seen the good-looking young man before but never in his dashing naval uniform. Because he was three years older, Rosalynn imagined that he thought of her as just a kid. One day when Jimmy asked her to the movies, she realized he liked her, too. They dated for a while, and when he returned to the naval academy in Annapolis, they exchanged letters. Soon their friendship ripened into love. When Jimmy came home at Christmas, he proposed. Rosalynn turned him down for two reasons:

*Rosalynn pins ensign bars on Jimmy during graduation day ceremonies at the U.S. Naval Academy.*

Rosalynn and Jimmy pose
on their wedding day.

she wanted to finish college, and she felt that her mother needed her at home. Rosalynn also suspected that Earl Carter, Jimmy's father, did not want his son to marry a Plains girl, but she was glad that his mother Lillian was fond of her.

By this time World War II had ended, and Rosalynn was grateful Jimmy would not be sent overseas to fight. In February, when he proposed again, the young woman accepted. On July 7, 1946, Rosalynn Smith and Jimmy Carter were married in a small private ceremony at the Methodist Church in Plains. Moving down the aisle, the bride's face was radiant with happiness as she looked forward to a life of fulfillment with the man she loved.

*Rosalynn is pictured here in 1960s with her sons Jack, Chip, and Jeff.*

# 2

# Mrs. Jimmy Carter

At first Rosalynn found it difficult to adjust to being a Navy wife. Stationed in Norfolk, Virginia, Jimmy's schedule kept him at sea five days a week. This made the nineteen-year-old bride unhappy, but she did her best to work things out. Soon she learned how to cook, pay bills, and cope with service people.

On July 3, 1947, Rosalynn gave birth to her first child, John William. The young mother loved little

Jack, as he was nicknamed. Because neither her mother or Jimmy's mother could be there to help, Jimmy requested two-week's leave and took care of his family until Rosalynn felt stronger.

In 1948 Jimmy was appointed to submarine school in New London, Connecticut. The Carters were given housing quarters on the base, and for the first time Jimmy kept normal hours. The couple was now able to have more of a social life and take courses in Spanish and art together.

Jimmy's next assignment was in Hawaii. Rosalynn loved the tropical climate and beauty so much, she never wanted to leave. On April 12, 1950, the Carter's second son, James Earl Carter III, was born and nicknamed Chip. Suddenly, the news broke about the United States entering the war in Korea, and Jimmy was ordered to San Diego.

Because of overcrowded conditions in San Diego, the Carters were forced to rent an apartment in a run-down neighborhood. Warned about the many bars in the area, Rosalynn locked the door whenever she went out to hang the laundry in the yard. To add to her misery, there was a nasty landlady who kept complaining that Mrs. Carter did not clean her apartment properly. After five months, Rosalynn was relieved when orders came through for Jimmy to return to New London. She made new friends among the other Navy wives and enjoyed the more relaxed lifestyle. The Carters purchased their first TV set, and the family watched baseball games together. On Rosalynn's twenty-fifth birthday, August 18, 1952, her third son, Jeff, was born.

One night Jimmy received a call that his father was dying from cancer. He went to Plains immediately and resigned from the Navy a few weeks later. When Jimmy insisted that they must return to Plains permanently so he could take care of the family's peanut business, Rosalynn was upset. She enjoyed the life of a Navy wife—seeing so many different places—and she didn't want to go back to her small hometown.

Back in Plains, they moved into a government housing project because Jimmy's Navy income had stopped. Rosalynn stayed busy sewing and reading and kept to herself. When Jimmy asked her to help in the peanut business, she was glad to relieve him of some of the work. Life in Plains became more interesting now. As business improved, they moved into a big old house on the edge of town. In the huge back yard the boys had more room to play, and Rosalynn loved the peaceful new surroundings.

In 1954 when the U.S. Supreme Court ordered integration in the public schools, Jimmy urged the local school board to cooperate. Many white people did not share his viewpoint. They didn't want black students to attend the same school as white students. As a member of the Lion's Club, the Chamber of Commerce, and other civic associations, Jimmy became increasingly involved in the racial issue. Although the Carters had accepted segregation when they were children, they now realized it was an unfair practice and wanted to do something about it. At the age of thirty-eight, Jimmy decided to run for the Georgia Senate. It was a hard battle but Jimmy Carter came out on top.

In 1966, Carter ran for Governor of Georgia. Rosalynn and her sons campaigned vigorously, but Jimmy lost the election to Lester Maddox. A former restaurant owner, Maddox had become famous for waving an ax handle at black customers who tried to eat in his restaurant. Refusing to accept defeat, Jimmy made plans to enter the next governor's race.

Rosalynn gave birth to their daughter, Amy, in 1967 but continued to work in her husband's behalf soon after. At first she found it difficult to speak before large crowds, but Rosalynn soon overcame her shyness as she traveled across the state, distributing

*Rosalynn holds two microphones as Jimmy and campaign workers celebrate his victory in the 1970 Georgia governor's race.*

brochures, shaking hands, and making speeches. Miss Lillian, brother Billy, and his wife, Sybil, as well as the Carter's sons and friends, all pitched in to help with the campaign. Sometimes, Rosalynn had to leave her young daughter with her mother. It was wrenching, but she knew Amy had the devoted care of a loving grandparent.

In 1970, Jimmy Carter ran for governor again, and this time he won. He was now the seventy-sixth governor of Georgia, and Rosalynn was the state's first lady. It was a hard-won victory. Rosalynn could scarcely believe it was true.

*In 1971, Rosalynn and Jimmy arrive at the governor's inaugural ball in Atlanta.*

# 3

# First Lady
# of Georgia

All the time she was campaigning, Rosalynn never stopped to think what life would be like in the Governor's Mansion. Nothing in her past had prepared her for planning formal receptions and training a large staff of servants. Once when the Carters were invited to an elegant dinner in the mansion of the governor of North Carolina, finger bowls appeared on the table. Rosalynn waited to see what the other guests did, then followed their example. In the following months, the new First Lady learned many things she never knew, and as time went on she became more confident.

The Governor's Mansion in Atlanta was a stately brick house with white columns surrounded by trees behind a tall, wrought-iron fence. The entrance was guarded by state patrolmen, and the interior was cared for by a staff of honor prisoners from the Georgia State Prison. Preparing for state functions might have become a full-time activity if Rosalynn had allowed it. Instead, she hired an experienced housekeeper who trained a member of the staff to be the cook. Sometimes the cook served special dishes to the family, and when they were perfected they were served to the guests.

So much entertaining required Rosalynn to have a large wardrobe. Not wanting to invest in a lot of formal wear, the women in the Carter family worked out a practical arrangement. Fortunately both Jack and Chip's wives and Jeff's girlfriend were the same size as their mother-in-law. The result was that the four women collected their evening clothes and kept them in a special closet that they called the gown room. This arrangement provided everyone something different to wear on formal occasions, especially the first lady. She got first choice.

*Rosalynn and Jimmy enjoy a quiet night at home with Amy.*

Rosalynn realized that guards were needed in the state mansion for security reasons, but she disliked being followed everywhere she went. She requested the guards who accompanied her outdoors to wear plain clothes so they wouldn't attract attention. This helped, although it did not always work.

When Amy played in the backyard, a guard was always nearby. Rosalynn couldn't believe family members needed so much protection, but one morning she changed her mind. As the Carters were eating breakfast, they saw an extra guard patrolling the French doors opening onto the porch. When Jimmy questioned the guard, he told the governor that there had been a serious threat on his life. Though Rosalynn was upset, Jimmy insisted on going to his office as usual. After this incident, whenever Rosalynn saw extra officers on patrol she worried but bravely followed her husband's example.

One of the prisoners working in the mansion was a young black woman who took care of Amy. Mary Fitzpatrick was devoted to the little girl, who loved her in return. When Rosalynn learned that Mary had been forced to plead guilty to a murder she hadn't committed, she decided to investigate. She learned that the court-appointed lawyer had convinced his client that pleading guilty would get her a lighter sentence. Young and penniless, Mary accepted what she was told and received a life sentence. Disturbed by this injustice, Rosalynn became involved in working with the Georgia Women's Prison Committee. She was also instrumental in obtaining better conditions and work release centers for women prisoners. After they left the Governor's Mansion, the Carters obtained justice for Amy's nanny by having her paroled and later pardoned.

Before long, the first lady turned to other projects in which she was interested. Concerned with the problems of the mentally handicapped, Rosalynn volunteered to help at one of the Georgia state mental hospitals. She became active in the Special Olympics, a program started by Eunice Kennedy Shriver. The Special Olympics encouraged mentally and physically handicapped people to compete in sporting events.

In the next three years, the Governor's Commission on Mental Health organized community health centers. These centers offered a place for mental patients who lived at home to have somewhere to go during the day. At the beginning of the Carter governorship there had been twenty-three mental health centers in the state. Under his administration they were increased to 134.

Another undertaking by Rosalynn was the beautification of Georgia roads and highways. Based on a similar program by former First Lady Ladybird Johnson in Texas, Rosalynn developed a successful Georgia Highway Wildflower campaign. When the Equal Rights Amendment (ERA) needed support she did not hesitate to speak openly in its favor because she believed that women, as well as men, should be guaranteed legal protection under the U.S. Constitution.

Under Georgia law, a governor could not serve a second term, so in 1975 Jimmy decided to run for president of the United States. When his mother, Miss Lillian, returned from doing volunteer work in the Peace Corps in India, her son told her about his plans to run for president. "President of what?" she asked.

It was true that many people had not heard of Jimmy Carter. Nevertheless, the Carter family and their friends worked tirelessly to spread the news about him. On December 12, 1974, Jimmy officially announced he would seek the Democratic party's nomination. Rosalynn could scarcely believe what was happening, but she was excited about her husband's decision.

*In 1977, Rosalynn speaks at a conference supporting the Equal Rights Amendment. She had long been a supporter of the proposed amendment to guarantee equal rights to women.*

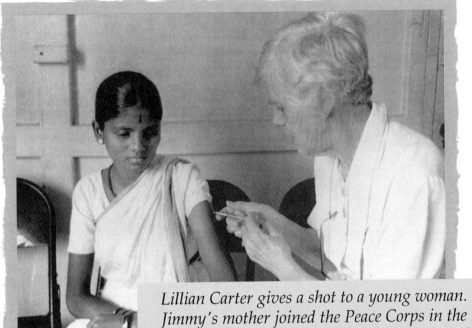

*Lillian Carter gives a shot to a young woman. Jimmy's mother joined the Peace Corps in the 1960s, working at a clinic in a small town in India. She was one of Rosalynn's closest friends.*

When Rosalynn had arrived at the Governor's Mansion in Atlanta, she had thought she would be returning to Plains after four years. Now everything was changed. As she listened to Jimmy's plans for the future, she realized their world would soon be moving beyond the limits of Georgia. From that moment on, Rosalynn Carter began to assume a vital role in helping Jimmy Carter become president of the United States.

*Rosalynn joins Jimmy and other family members at an appearance during Jimmy's 1976 presidential campaign.*

# 4

# The Road to
# the White House

During the next eighteen months, Rosalynn and Jimmy frequently traveled in different directions on the campaign trail. They spoke to people, shook hands, and answered questions. It was like the governor's campaign, only more demanding.

Rosalynn visited radio and TV stations and offered to be interviewed. Some of the talk-show hosts wondered what the attractive, soft-spoken woman had to say. When the interviewers did not know what questions to ask, Rosalynn handed them a list that she had prepared. The answers told the public who Jimmy was and what he stood for.

Sometimes Rosalynn traveled with Edna Langford, the mother of her daughter-in-law, Judy. Together they campaigned in different areas of the country. By the time the campaign was over, they had covered forty-two states.

One day on the road, Rosalynn's luggage was stolen. The only clothes she had were the ones she was wearing. There was no time to shop for another wardrobe. Using the hotel bathroom sink, Rosalynn laundered her single outfit, hung it up to dry, and emerged the next morning looking immaculate.

Whenever possible, Rosalynn arranged to get back to Plains for a weekend. Things had changed dramatically since she lived there. Secret Service agents, reporters, and tourists seemed to be everywhere. Hoping to see the Carters in person, people in cars, buses, and on foot tried to get close to the house on Woodland Drive. Rosalynn managed to set aside some time to be with Amy, but it was never enough. Although the Secret Service agents tried to disperse the curious crowds, they weren't always successful.

Aside from a few hectic situations, Rosalynn enjoyed the challenge of campaigning. She liked to visit with people and discuss their problems. In Iowa, Rosalynn talked with farmers. In Pennsylvania, she talked with coal miners. She visited nursing homes, mental health centers, shoe factories, and steel mills. When Rosalynn saw Jimmy she passed information on to him. In this way, they both learned more about the problems of Americans across the country.

As the months passed, the Carters sons and daughters-in-law, along with other campaign workers, toured different states raising money for the campaign. Paying their own way, a group of loyal Georgians called the Peanut Brigade covered the country telling Americans about the man they believed should be president. In January 1976, a hundred Georgians chartered a plane to New Hampshire. Once there, they knocked on doors, distributed brochures, and talked up a storm about their candidate.

In the state of Illinois, a problem arose when Jimmy wanted to appear on the ballot as "Jimmy Carter," but election officials insisted on using his full name, James Earl Carter Jr. The issue was settled by getting an official document from the state of Georgia that showed the name of Jimmy Carter had always been used for election purposes and, therefore, was legal.

Soon, Jimmy started receiving strong competition from other candidates who were better known than him. George Wallace, Henry "Scoop" Jackson, Jerry Brown, and Lloyd Bentsen, among others, were favorite sons in their own regions. Jimmy had to beat not just one of these men but all of them. It would not be easy.

The last weeks of the primaries were full of tension for Rosalynn. She did her best to smile in public, but when she was alone she prayed she would remain strong and not lose faith. Prayer always stood Rosalynn in good stead. On June 8, 1976, exhausted but hopeful, the Carter family met in Atlanta to await the final returns from three big states. When the news broke that had Jimmy won enough delegates to become the Democratic candidate for president, their friends all rejoiced with them.

Now Jimmy started to interview candidates for vice president. After many interviews, he finally chose Senator Walter "Fritz" Mondale of Minnesota as his running mate. In July 1976, the Carters arrived in New York to attend the Democratic National Convention.

*Walter and Joan Mondale and Jimmy and Rosalynn Carter*
*wave to the crowd at the 1976 Democratic Convention.*

All during their stay, security guards followed the Carters everywhere. Sometimes Rosalynn's friend Edna, or her secretary, Madeline, couldn't get into the Americana Hotel to see her. Once when Rosalynn took Amy to Central Park, the crowd of spectators became so large that the guards whisked mother and daughter right back to the hotel.

Although Rosalynn was sure that Jimmy would win, the night of the Democratic Convention found her "with butterflies in my stomach." Later she said it was also "one of the most thrilling moments of my life." A few hours later Jimmy Carter was officially nominated as the Democratic candidate.

*On election night, the Carter family celebrates Jimmy's victory in the presidential election.*

Being nominated was a tremendous thrill, but there was still a long way to go. Gerald Ford, the incumbent president and Republican nominee, was better known than Georgia's ex-governor. Were the American people ready for a change? This important question would be answered three months later in the general election.

Considered an essential part of the campaign, Rosalynn was now provided with a private jet.

Traveling with Secret Service agents and secretaries, she frequently covered six states in a day. Once off the plane, Rosalynn attended endless rallies and meetings. It was exciting but exhausting. Still, she did not slow down.

When the media called her "the Steel Magnolia," Jimmy was upset by it but not Rosalynn. "Steel is tough and magnolia is southern," she said. "I don't mind being described that way."

On Election Day, November 2, 1976, the Carter family waited for the results in an Atlanta hotel. The phones kept ringing constantly. Rosalynn and Jimmy paced back and forth trying to smile at each other encouragingly. They knew that election nights were tense, but this one seemed to be the worst. Rosalynn put Amy to bed and sat up with Jimmy until 3 a.m. Just as her eyelids began to droop, the phone rang loudly again. The voice on the other end shouted out the exciting news: Jimmy Carter had been declared the victor, amassing a total electoral-college vote of 272. The long struggle was over. Tears slipping down her cheeks, Rosalynn embraced the new president of the United States. A moment later the president-elect reminded Mrs. Carter she would be the first lady!

*On January 20, 1977, Rosalynn holds a Bible as Jimmy takes the presidential oath of office from Chief Justice Warren Burger.*

# 5

# 1600 Pennsylvania Avenue

January 20, 1977, was a sunny but freezing cold day in Washington, D.C. The weather did not stop the Carters from walking with their boys and a bundled-up Amy a mile and a half from the Capitol to the White House after the inauguration. It was the first time a president and his family had made such a journey.

That evening, wearing the same blue gown that she had worn at the Georgia inaugural ball six years earlier, Rosalynn danced with Jimmy at several inauguration celebrations. The next day, weary but exhilarated, the Carters settled into their new home at 1600 Pennsylvania Avenue.

With her sons, their wives, and Amy in their own rooms on the second and third floors of the big house, Rosalynn began to feel comfortable. In February when Amy's nanny, Mary, was paroled and came to care for the little girl, there wasn't a happier nine year-old in town.

Not wishing to spend most of her time as a hostess, the new first lady turned the arrangements for formal receptions over to the White House staff. This made it easier for Rosalynn to work on her own projects and to learn more about the presidency and share it with Jimmy.

When the Carters decided to send their daughter to a public school, the media gave the event maximum attention. On her first day at Stevens Elementary School, Amy was greeted by a crowd of reporters and TV cameras. Her new classmates stared at Amy and the Secret Service agents following her.

*Jimmy and Rosalynn wave to the crowd during Jimmy's inaugural parade.*

*In New York City's Central Park, Rosalynn and Amy pose in front of the Alice In Wonderland statue.*

After a while the fourth graders accepted the situation, and the new girl was able to make friends. In the spring, the Carters had a tree house built on the South Lawn. Sometimes on a warm evening Amy invited a friend to sleep over.

Because she was interested, Rosalynn began attending cabinet meetings and taking notes. When the press found out, they started a rumor that Rosalynn was telling Jimmy what to do. Nothing could have been further from the truth. Jimmy encouraged Rosalynn's interest, and they discussed things, but he always made up his own mind. In the East Wing of the White House, the first lady had her own office where she worked every day.

Soon after the inauguration, Jimmy asked Rosalynn to undertake a special mission. He wanted her to be his representative to Latin America and establish cordial relations with leaders in Brazil, Colombia, Costa Rica, and other countries. Rosalynn agreed and immediately began brushing up on her Spanish and knowledge of each country. With two months to prepare, the first lady had many hours of briefing from State Department officials and scholars on Latin affairs. She was also warned that Latin

*In Bolivia, Rosalynn shakes hands during her 1977 trip to Latin America.*

countries did not believe women should be involved in politics, but this did not stop her.

In June 1977, accompanied by state officials, a nurse, two secretaries, and Secret Service agents, Rosalynn traveled for two weeks, meeting with Latin American heads of state. Every night she talked on the phone with Jimmy to keep him informed of her progress. Rosalynn communicated well with different heads of state and generally received a warm response. On her return, Jimmy told Rosalynn that she had made an excellent goodwill ambassador and that he was proud of her.

Even before the Latin American tour Rosalynn started off on her first major public project. As honorary chairperson of the President's Commission on Mental Health from 1977–78, she developed a program to improve services to people suffering from mental illnesses and prompted passage of the Mental Health Systems Act.

In September 1978, Rosalynn accompanied Jimmy to Camp David, the presidential retreat in Maryland, to take part in a history-making event. Jimmy's purpose in meeting with President Anwar al-Sadat of Egypt and Prime Minister Menachem

Begin of Israel was to bring peace to the Middle East. Rosalynn soon developed a positive relationship with the two leaders and their wives. The Camp David meeting led to the signing of a peace agreement between Israel and Egypt. Because it brought to an end the state of war between the two countries, the agreement was considered one of Jimmy's outstanding presidential achievements.

In October 1979, Jimmy Carter gave permission for Shah Mohammed Reza Pahlavi to enter the United States. The controversial former leader of Iran was suffering from cancer. Despite Iranian threats, Carter felt the humane thing was to allow the sick man treatment. The following month, Iranian student demonstrators seized the U.S. Embassy in Teheran, demanding the return of the Shah and multimillion-dollar fortune. With the support of the Iranian government, the demonstrators held fifty-two U.S. citizens hostage for 444 days. Carter worked hard to gain their release and was finally successful on his last day in office. The hostages were released minutes after he turned the office of president over to Ronald Reagan, who had defeated him in the 1980 presidential election.

*In January 1978, Rosalynn and Jimmy greet guests at the White House.*

*During the 1980 presidential campaign,
Rosalynn speaks to voters in Waterloo, Iowa.*

On January 20, 1981, the Carters returned to their home in Plains. No longer were they in the center of exciting Washington life. Years stretched ahead of them living in a town they had only visited in years. Rosalynn wondered what she would do with the rest of her life. It did not take her long to find out.

*The Carters give Nancy and Ronald Reagan a guided tour of the Carter Presidential Library.*

# 6

# Always Involved

For a short while, the Carters relaxed. Jimmy worked in his woodshop, and Rosalynn planted a vegetable garden. They rode their bikes and walked in the woods. In the north Georgia mountains, they built a log cabin that had a waterfall in the front yard. Friends and family came to visit, including the grandchildren who were old enough to travel.

The Carters traveled to China, Japan, the Middle East, Australia, and other parts of the world.

When publishers asked them to write books, Rosalynn and Jimmy were delighted. It took Jimmy a year to write his memoirs, *Keeping Faith* (1982). Rosalynn took longer to complete her best-selling autobiography, *First Lady From Plains* (1984). She was still troubled about Jimmy's 1980 defeat, but as always her strong religious faith helped her cope.

Before long the Carters became involved in planning and building a presidential library. They found a favorable site for it in Atlanta and set about raising the needed funds for this project. When it was dedicated in 1986, they felt they had established a worthwhile source for research about the Carter presidency and its achievements Another building, the James Earl Carter Library, was founded on the campus of Georgia Southwestern College, Rosalynn's alma mater, now known as Georgia Southwestern State University. This library is a study center holding the president's papers, pictures, and family memorabilia.

When Jimmy was offered a position as an instructor at Emory University, he was glad to accept because he always wanted to teach. Busy as the

Carters were with their writing and other activities, Rosalynn felt there was still more to do. There were vital problems to research and people to help. It was time to get started.

In 1982, Rosalynn and Jimmy founded the Carter Center in Atlanta. They made it "a place where people could come together to resolve their differences." Their purpose was to advance the cause of peace and human rights around the world. In many developing countries, the Center is teaching farmers to grow more crops and working to fight terrible diseases. The Center also encourages democracy by overseeing elections and trying to resolve conflicts and wars in these countries. Rosalynn continues to work with Jimmy on all these issues.

Rosalynn also started her own projects at the Carter Center, among them the Rosalynn Carter Symposium on Mental Health. Members of her Mental Health Task Force strive to bring about better conditions for victims of mental illness. They also work to help the elderly and promote improved living conditions for the homeless.

One week each summer, Rosalynn and Jimmy volunteer to build homes for the poor in different

U.S. cities. This project—Habitat for Humanity—continues to this day with volunteers not only in the United States but also in many other countries around the world. Onlookers are thrilled by the sight of the former president and first lady on their hands and knees sawing, sanding, and painting.

In 1987, Rosalynn co-authored a book with Jimmy titled *Everything to Gain: Making the Most of the Rest of Your Life*. This book describes how life after the White House and growing older did not prevent the Carters from experiencing additional productive years. Though they had problems to overcome like any other couple, they welcomed this part of living as a beginning rather than an end.

Today, as a grandmother of nine, Rosalynn continues to be concerned about her own mother. Allie Smith, now in her nineties, enjoys good health and still lives in Plains, where Rosalynn gets to see her frequently. Because she became concerned about her mother's welfare, Rosalynn began to realize how important it is to provide for the needs of elderly people. She felt that adult children and relatives play a significant role as caregivers, especially for physically, mentally disabled, and frail elderly people. As

*In 1987, Rosalynn autographs a copy of the book that she coauthored with Jimmy,* Everything to Gain: Making the Most of the Rest of Your Life.

*As volunteers for Habitat for Humanity, Rosalynn and Jimmy help build a house. Rosalynn remains active in many social and humanitarian causes.*

a result, after much investigation and research, Rosalynn wrote a book on the topic. *Helping Yourself Help Others*, co-authored with Susan K. Galant, was published in 1994.

Working on behalf of important social causes has become one of the major aspects of Rosalynn Carter's life. In 1991 she developed a nationwide campaign called Every Child By Two. This program emphasized the need for children to receive age-appropriate immunization against childhood diseases.

Over the years the former first lady has received numerous honors for her outstanding work. Among them are the Volunteer of the Decade Award from the National Mental Health Association, the Award of Merit for the Support of the Equal Rights Amendment from the National Organization of Women, and the Notre Dame Award for International Service.

In recent years, there has been sadness as well as joy in the Carter household. The passing of two of the people Rosalynn loved dearly—Miss Lillian, and her best friend, Ruth—left a painful void. The Carter sons are involved in various professions and as parents to Rosalynn's grandchildren. While she attended Brown University, Amy Carter became involved in different causes. She later graduated from Memphis College of Art in Tennessee. When she returned to Atlanta, Amy found a job in a bookstore. There, she met and fell in love with James Wentzel, a computer consultant. On September 1, 1996, the young couple were married in Plains, Georgia.

In between speaking engagements, book signings, research, and conferences, Rosalynn enjoys biking, jogging, and fly-fishing with Jimmy. She continues to accompany her husband on all of his peace missions around the world. In her late sixties, Rosalynn Carter continues to display extraordinary energy and drive, and the same warm smile lights up her face when she speaks.

Some first ladies have played more of a role in their husband's presidencies than others. Rosalynn Carter was an active member of Jimmy Carter's presidential team, and she always managed to maintain her individual integrity and independence. Born in a tiny rural town, Rosalynn rose to one of the most prominent positions in the United States. For those who wonder about the "steel" in the image of the Steel Magnolia, Rosalynn Carter explains it simply, "I do and I say what I think is right, but I always have prayed about it first."

Looking forward to the twenty-first century, the former first lady continues to promote the humanitarian causes that are so important to her. Rosalynn Carter has touched many lives. She is a role model for young and old alike, a first lady to be remembered.

# ℱor more information

**For Further Reading**

Carter, Jimmy. *Talking Peace*. New York: Dutton, 1993.

Quiri, Patricia Ryon. *The White House*. Danbury, CT: Franklin Watts, 1996.

Sandak, Cass A. *The Carters*. New York: Crestwood House, 1993.

Wade, Linda R. *James Carter*. Chicago: Children's Press, 1989.

**For Advanced Readers**

Carter, Jimmy. *Keeping Faith*. New York: Bantam, 1982.

Carter, Jimmy and Rosalynn Carter. *Everything to Gain: Making the Most of the Rest of Your Life*. New York: Random House, 1987.

Carter, Rosalynn. *First Lady from Plains*. New York: Fawcett, 1985.

Slavin, Ed. *Jimmy Carter*. New York: Chelsea House, 1989.

Smith, Betsy C. *Jimmy Carter, President*. New York Walker, 1986.

**Internet Sites**

Because of the changeable nature of the internet, sites appear and disappear very quickly. These resources offered useful information on Rosalynn Carter at the time of publication. Internet addresses must be entered with capital and lowercase letters exactly as they appear.

http://www.yahoo.com

The Yahoo directory of the World Wide Web is an excellent place to find internet sites on any topic.

http://www.emory.edu/CARTER_CENTER/
This is the home page for the Carter Center, the private, nonprofit institution founded by the Carters in 1982. It has lots of information on Rosalynn, Jimmy, and the programs supported by the Carter Center.

http:gswrs6k1.gsw.peachnet.edu/Carter/carter.html
This is the home page of the Rosalynn Carter Institute of Southwest Georgia College.

http://www.habitat.org
This is the home page of the Habitat for Humanity, a network of volunteers who build homes for the needy.

# $\mathcal{I}$ndex

# About the Author

Ruth Turk, a former English teacher, is a writer and lecturer. She has written eighteen books for young readers, including biographies of Lillian Hellman, Ray Charles, and Charlie Chaplin. Ms. Turk lives in Lake Worth, Florida.